Dedicated to my sister Lori who asked me a simple question that changed my entire world view.

Thank you!

Copyright Information

Title: Who made you? God or goo?

Author: Carrie Hernández

Publisher: Matthew 10:32 Publishing

Contact: contact@knowingjesuslovingjesus.com

HAVE YOU EVER WONDERED,
AT THE WONDERS,
OF LIFE AND EARTH AND SUN?

HAVE YOU EVER PAUSED,
TO FIND THE CAUSE,
OF LIFE IN EVERYONE?

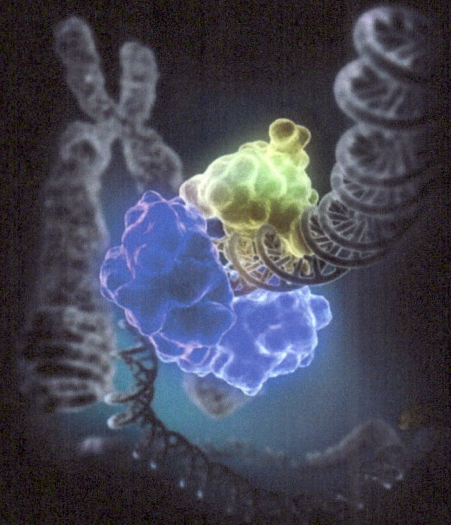

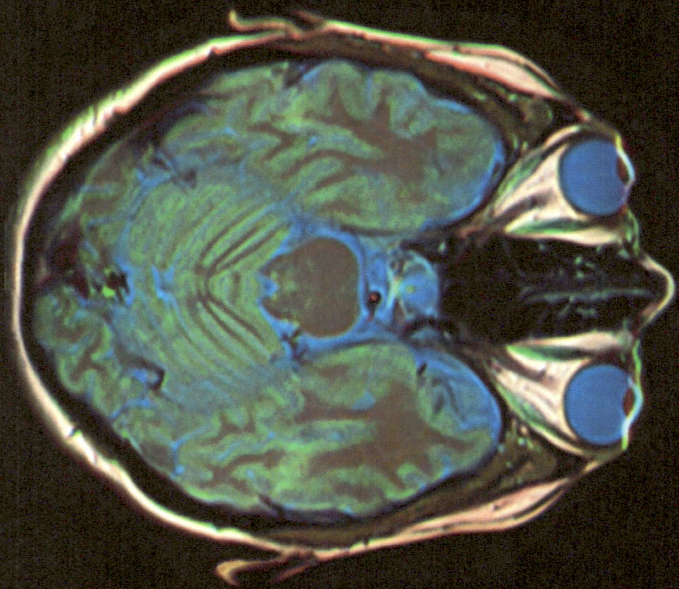

OTHERS HAVE THOUGHT, AND THOUGHT,
AND THOUGHT, OF HOW THIS LIFE COULD BE.

THEY WANTED TO KNOW, AND TEACH, AND SHOW,
THE METHOD TO YOU AND ME.

THEY STRAINED THEIR BRAINS,
AND THEN EXCLAIMED,
"NOW I KNOW THE WAY!"

THEIR THOUGHTS GREW HAZY,
OR THEY WENT CRAZY,
BUT THIS IS WHAT
THEY SAY...

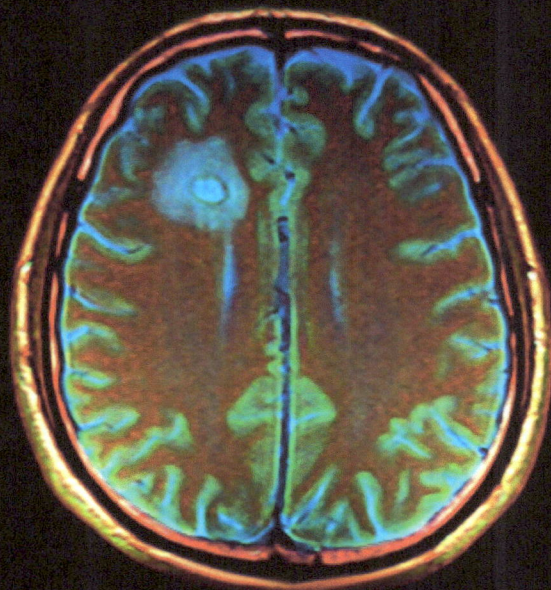

THEY TRY TO SHOW, THAT LONG AGO,
WATER DRIPPED ON ROCK.

AND FOUR HUNDRED MILLION
(NOW UP TO 4.6 BILLION),
YEARS HAVE PASSED UPON THE CLOCK.

THEY SAY THEY FOUND, ROCK MELTED DOWN,
AND FORMED SOME CRAZY goo.

THEN THEY SAID,
THAT goo IT SPREAD,
AND TURNED TO
ME AND YOU.

THEY KINDA THOUGHT,
THAT goo GOT SHOCKED,
BY LIGHTNING FROM THE SKY.

AND THEN KABLAME,
THE goo BECAME,
MAGICALLY ALIVE.

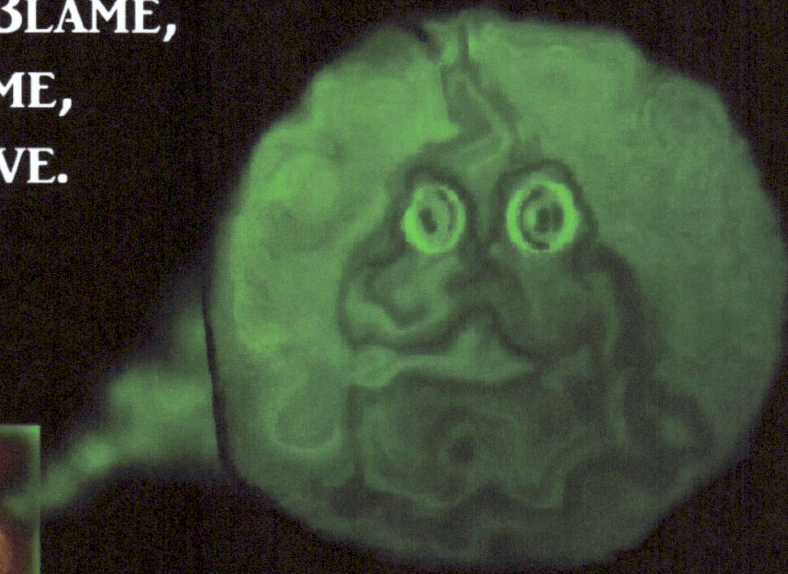

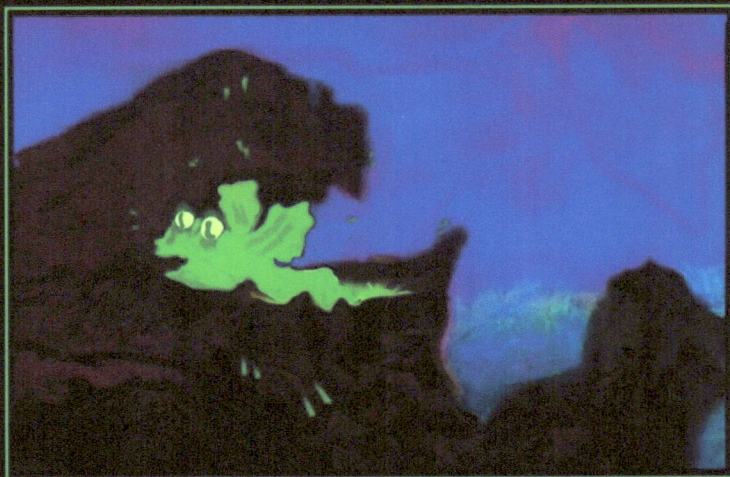

MORE TIME WENT BY, THE goo SURVIVED,
THOUGH NONE CAN TELL YOU WHY,

THE goo IT SPREAD, AND IT FORMED A HEAD,
AND THEN IT LEARNED TO FLY.

BY NOW THE goo, HAD TURNED INTO,
SOMETHING CALLED A BIRD.

AND HERE WE GO, IT CHANGES MORE,
AND THOUGH IT SOUNDS ABSURD...

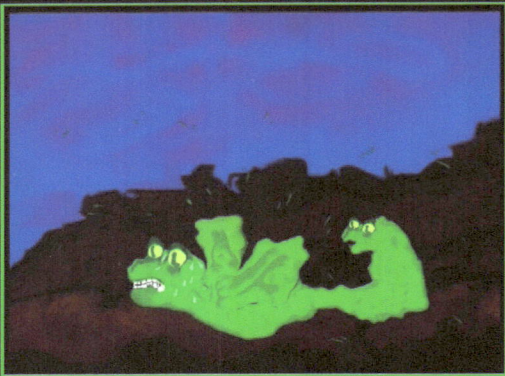
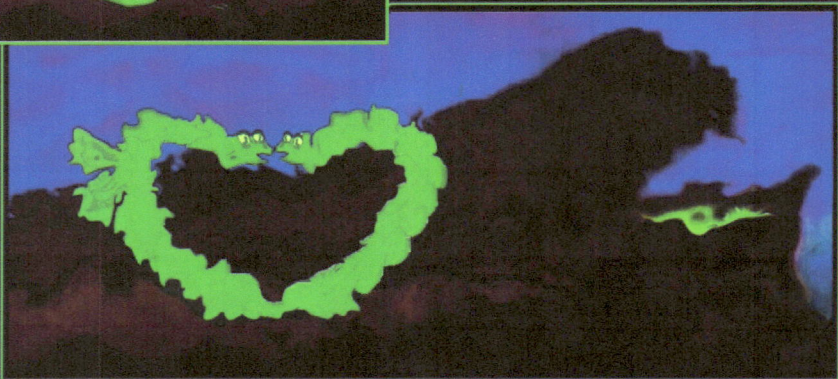
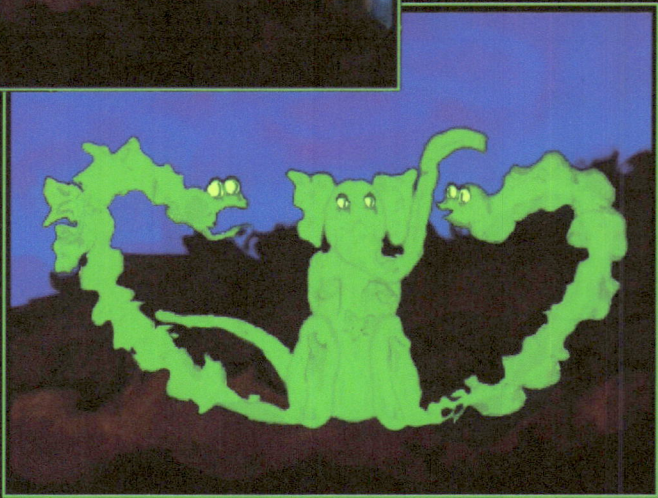

THAT goo, IT MADE,
NOT ONE BUT TWO,
AND THOSE TWO MADE
A BABY.

AND THAT BABY,
MADE A BABY,
AND THAT BABY,
MADE A MAYBE.

AND THE MAYBE,
WAS A NEW
KIND OF goo,
MAYBE AN ELEPHANT,
MAYBE A KANGAROO.

AND THE NEW goo GREW,
AND TIME SURE FLEW,
AND THEN IT CHANGED INTO...

A NEWER goo,
THAT BECAME,
A NEWER goo,
THAT BECAME,
AN EVEN NEWER goo.

AND THEN KABLAME,
THE goo BECAME, EVERYONE YOU KNOW.

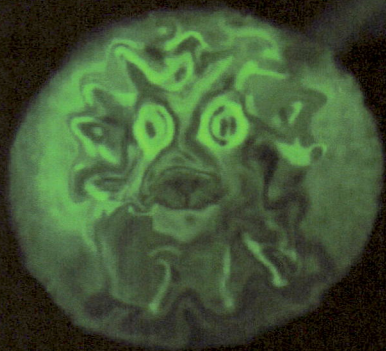

AND IF THIS THEORY WEREN'T WEIRD,
AND THE goo HAD PERSEVERED,
THEN WE'D SAY "WAY TO GO!"

FOR ROCK AND RAIN ARE NOT THE SAME,
THEY MELTED INTO goo ,
AND THEN THE goo IT GREW AND GREW,
AND GREW AND GREW AND GREW,
AND NOW IT THINKS IT'S YOU.

AND DON'T FORGET,
AS WELL AS YOU,
IT TURNED INTO...
EVERY ANIMAL AT THE ZOO!

WHEW!
THAT goo SURE GREW.

"THIS IS NUTS", YOU STOP AND SAY, "I DO NOT UNDERSTAND.
HOW SOME goo, FROM ROCK AND RAIN
HAS TURNED INTO, A MAN!"

NOW SOME WILL SAY,
THAT GOD STEPPED IN,
AND USED THAT goo LIKE CLAY.
AND SLOWLY, SLOWLY, SLOWLY, SLOWLY,
GUIDED IT ON ITS WAY.

BUT HERE'S THE QUESTION BOYS AND GIRLS,
HERE'S THE PROBLEM I FIND.
DOES GOD WITH ALL HIS KNOWLEDGE AND POWER,
REALLY NEED THE TIME?

AND IF I KNOW THAT WITHOUT MY GOD,
THE goo TO YOU IS SILLY.
OF COURSE I KNOW, THE goo DIDN'T GROW
TO A PERSON WILLY NILLY.

IT'S SO ODD, THAT IT MUST BE GOD,
HE HELPED IT FORM AND GROW.
THEY'LL SAY TO YOU, THAT GOD USED goo,
VERY, VERY SLOW.

HERE'S MY PROBLEM, LISTEN CLOSE, THE goo NEEDS GOD TO THRIVE.
BUT WHY, OH WHY, DO WE THINK GOD,
NEEDS goo TO MAKE HIS WORLD ALIVE?

NOW I DO NOT SAY, THAT THERE'S NO WAY,
THAT GOD COULD MAKE THIS WORK.
IF GOD SO CHOSE, WITH THE POWER HE SHOWS,
HE COULD FORM US OUT OF MURK.

BUT WHY DO WE SAY,
THIS IS THE WAY,
THAT IT HAD TO GO?
WHY DO WE TELL,
THIS CRAZY TALE,
AND SAY IT HAPPENED SLOW.

WHY DO WE,
TRY TO BELIEVE,
IN THIS gooey STORY?
WHY DON'T WE,
LOOK AND SEE,

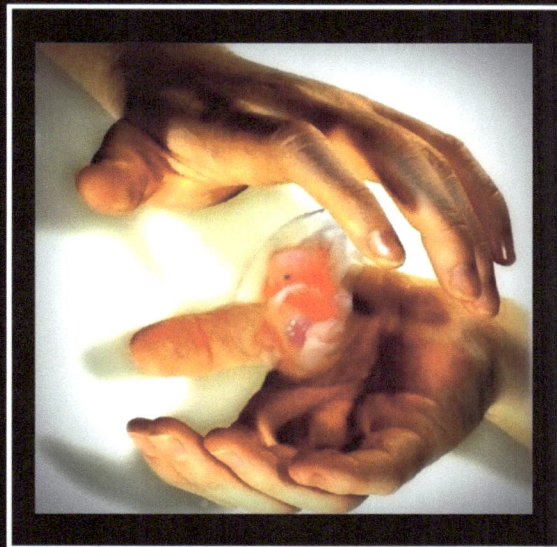

The story of the goo,
is man's attempt to explain to you,
how life could arise,
Without GOD, with out a guide,
without someone so wise.

But since we know that GOD is there,
and that he cares,
and that He caused our life to be,
Why don't we admit that GOD
simply created you and me?

When we know that GOD exists,
why do we still try,
To tell the world that it must be GOD
that made the goo alive?

Let me tell you, one and all,
that **GOD** said how He did it.
He made the earth,
He made the heavens,
and then He formed us in it.

GOD says He did it in six days,
with awesome might and power.
He made a sea, He made a me,
He made a gorgeous flower.

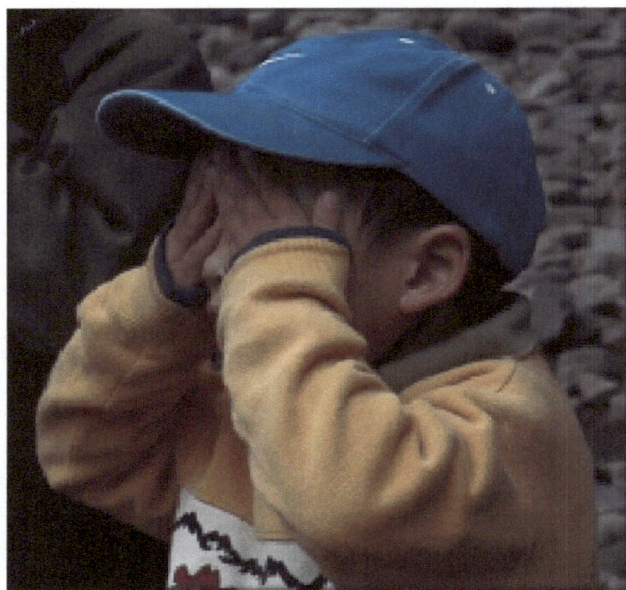

YET THERE ARE PEOPLE WHO,
HOPE **GOD**'S EXISTENCE ISN'T TRUE,
SO THEY SCRAMBLE TO DENY.

THEY HUNT AND SEARCH,
REFUSING CHURCH
AND THEY KEEP ON GUESSING WHY.

THEY TWIST AND BEND
AND STRETCH THE TRUTH
TILL ALL THAT'S LEFT ARE LIES.

THEY EXPLAIN THE WORLD,
AND LIFE AND WONDERS,
WHILE COVERING THEIR EYES.

What a foolish mistake,
the time they waste,
developing this theory.
The answers written,
for all who'll listen,
the bible tells us clearly.

We already know, the way it goes,
that GOD made me and you.
So we refuse, to sit and muse,
that there's any truth,

In a theory,
that states quite clearly,
that once upon a time – we were
goo.

What do you think is true?

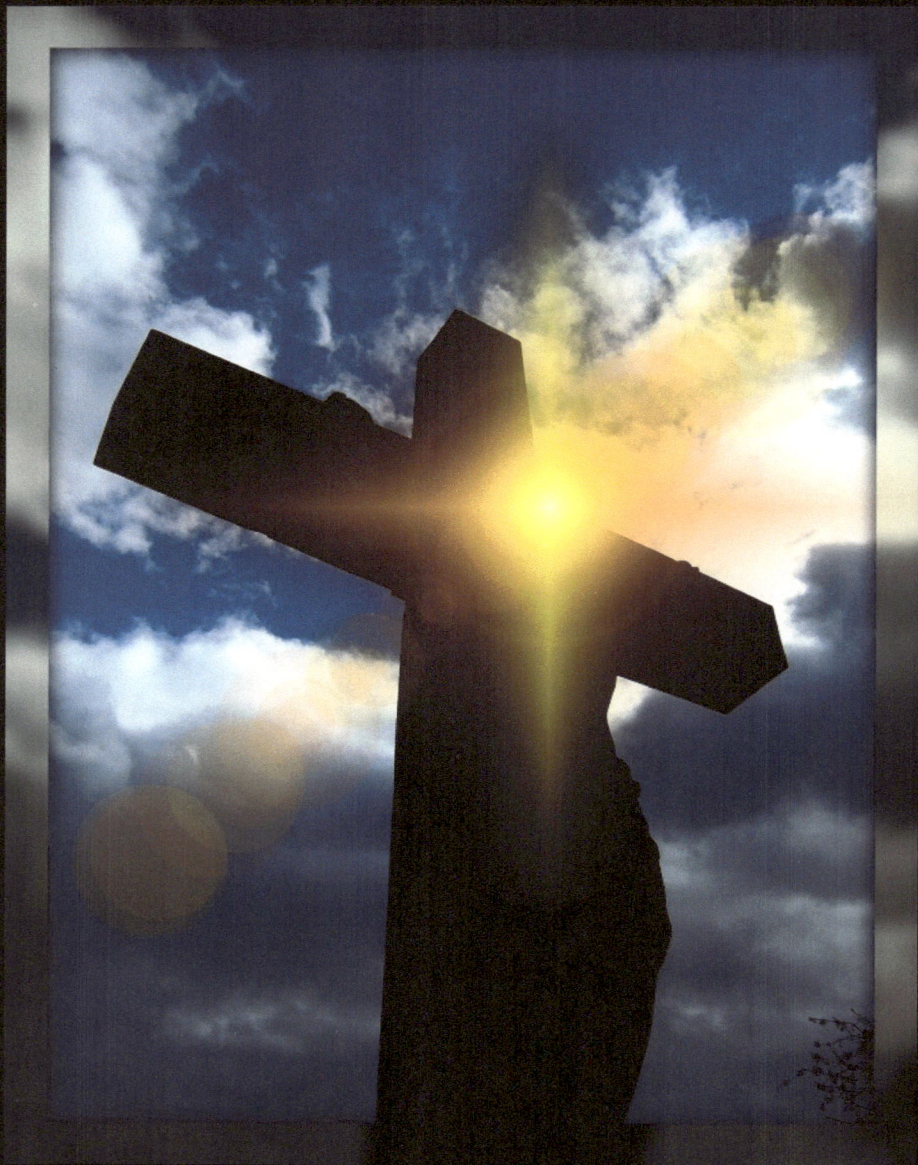

19 because what may be known of God is manifest in them, for God has shown it to them.

20 For since the creation of the world His invisible attributes are clearly seen, being understood by the things that are made, even His eternal power and Godhead, so that they are without excuse,

21 because, although they knew God, they did not glorify Him as God, nor were thankful, but became futile in their thoughts, and their foolish hearts were darkened.

22 Professing to be wise, they became fools,

23 and changed the glory of the incorruptible God into an image made like corruptible man--and birds and four-footed animals and creeping things.

24 Therefore God also gave them up to uncleanness, in the lusts of their hearts, to dishonor their bodies among themselves,

25 who exchanged the truth of God for the lie, and worshiped and served the creature rather than the Creator, who is blessed forever. Amen.

Romans 1:19-25 NKJV

Ready, Set, goo!

Supply List:

- Adult supervision
- Stove
- Sauce pan
- Whisk
- Spatula
- 1 cup flour
- 1 cup water
- 1/4 cup salt
- 2 tablespoons oil
- 1 tablespoon cream of tartar
- 1 package of sugar-free jello

Mix the ingredients in sauce pan and whisk away any clumps. Place on low heat. Stir frequently. Cook for 5-7 minutes, stirring with a spatula. Once the dough starts to gather into a ball (see the picture) you can take it off the stove. After it is cool enough to handle, knead it on a cutting board.

That's all there is to making goo!

Questions to ask a younger child

1. Ask your child if the goo can tweet or hop or fly.
2. Toss it up and catch it and show it will not fly.
3. Form it into a bird and ask the child if that bird could make a baby bird.

If they say yes let them show you and then explain that they made the baby bird from the goo. That it wasn't the goo bird that made the baby bird.

4. Ask them if they think that the goo bird is alive.
5. Ask them if they think that the goo bird could grow into a person.

Wait a minute watching the goo bird. Wait for it to transform. Then suddenly squish the goo bird down and make it into a person. Explain that you had to make it just like God had to make us. The goo can't change its shape on its own.

6. Ask them if they think that the goo person is alive. Does it breathe? Move? Think?
7. Ask them if they think that they could make the goo person turn into a real person.

Explain to them that after God formed man he breathed into his nostrils the breath of life and only after God gave us the breath of life did we become a living soul. Explain that only God can create life.

QUESTIONS TO ASK AN OLDER CHILD.

1. ASK YOUR CHILD WHAT THEY KNOW ABOUT GOD AS OUR CREATOR.

2. ASK YOUR CHILD WHAT THEY KNOW ABOUT EVOLUTION.

3. ASK YOUR CHILD IF THEY THINK THAT NON-LIVING MATTER CAN COME ALIVE.

4. ASK YOUR CHILD IF THEY THINK A REPTILE CAN TURN INTO A BIRD.

IF THEY SAY YES, TALK TO THEM ABOUT HOW COMPLEX FLIGHT IS AND HOW AN ANIMAL HALF WAY BETWEEN A LIZARD AND A BIRD WOULDN'T BE ABLE TO RUN BUT ALSO WOULDN'T BE ABLE TO FLY. HOW WOULD IT SURVIVE? HOW DID THE BONES, LUNGS, HEART, AND WINGS ALL CHANGE TO SUPPORT FLIGHT BEFORE FLYING WOULD HAVE BEEN BENEFICIAL?

5. ASK THE CHILD IF A BIRD CAN TURN INTO ANOTHER KIND OF BIRD.

IF THEY SAY YES, AGREE. IF THEY SAY NO, DISAGREE. GOD CREATED ALL ANIMALS ACCORDING TO THEIR KINDS AND GAVE THEM THE ABILITY TO BE FRUITFUL AND MULTIPLY OVER THE FACE OF THE EARTH. THIS MEANS THAT ANIMALS CAN ADAPT TO THEIR ENVIRONMENT. ADAPTATION (ALSO KNOWN AS MICROEVOLUTION) IS NOT ONLY POSSIBLE IT MAKES THE NUMBER OF ANIMALS FOR NOAH'S ARK VERY REASONABLE.

6. ASK THE CHILD IF THEY THINK THAT IF YOU HAD ALL THE BUILDING BLOCKS OF LIFE IN A GLASS OF WATER THAT LIFE WOULD EVENTUALLY COME OUT OF THE GLASS.

IF THEY SAY YES, FIND A DEAD BUG AND PUT IT IN A GLASS OF WATER. A BUG HAS ALL THE BUILDING BLOCKS OF LIFE. ADD ENERGY BY PUTTING IT IN THE MICROWAVE OR PLACING A LID ON IT AND SHAKING. SEE IF THE BUG COMES BACK TO LIFE. A BUG HAS ALL THE BUILDING BLOCKS OF LIFE ALREADY ARRANGED IN THE PROPER ORDER. IF THE BUG CAN'T COME BACK TO LIFE AND CRAWL OUT OF THE WATER WHAT MAKES THEM THINK THAT A GERM COULD FORM ITSELF AND CRAWL OUT? *

7. ASK THE CHILD IF THEY WERE ASKED TO DECIDE WHO WAS TELLING THE TRUTH AND ONE PERSON KEPT CHANGING THEIR STORY AND THE OTHER PERSON'S VERSION WAS ALWAYS THE SAME, WHO WOULD THEY BELIEVE?

EXPLAIN THAT THE 'PROOFS' OF EVOLUTION ARE DISPROVEN ON A REGULAR BASIS AND THAT THE EVOLUTIONISTS JUST CHANGE THEIR THEORY. THE THEORY IS BEING CONSTANTLY REVISED AS OLD IDEAS ARE PROVEN WRONG AND NEW 'PROOFS' ARE FOUND. YET GOD'S VERSION OF CREATION NEVER WAVERS.

* PLEASE MAKE SURE THE BUG IS REALLY DEAD BEFORE YOU BEGIN!

There will be questions that come up as your child goes through school that you will not have a ready answer for:

Simply look them up together. Make it a family activity.

Discuss how and why scientists may have come to the wrong conclusion based on their assumptions.

Answersingenesis.org is a fantastic resource for all ages.

And since there will be challenging questions for you to answer I thought I'd provide some challenging questions your children can ask their teachers.

Questions your children can ask their teachers as they progress through school

~ If your kids ask, other kids may learn the truth~

1.   How did nothing explode, nowhere, before time existed and create a universe with matter, space, and time?

2.   The laws of science contain many numbers, like the size of the electrical charge of the atoms and force of gravity that if changed even a little would mean life couldn't exist. If there is no God who fine-tuned the universe so we could live?

3.   Why won't the earth and the sun cooperate with the predictions of science?
https://answersingenesis.org/kids/astronomy/the-planets-wont-cooperate/

4.   How did the amino acid building blocks that turn into proteins form on their own?

5.   How did the amino acids become a protein without DNA to guide it? The probability of this happening is 1 in 10300 but 1 in 1050 is considered mathematically impossible.

6.   What came first the DNA or a cell?

7.   DNA is like the instruction manual for the body. Who wrote the manual?

8.   The cell is more complicated than a rocket ship. How did the first cell 'figure' out how to feed itself.

9.   What did it eat?

10.   How did it figure out how to make a copy of itself?

11.   How did it learn to make itself into other kinds of cells?

12.   Why did it decide that sometimes it would need another cell just like it to make babies?

13.   How did the first pair of creatures that needed two to make a baby find each other.

14.   How did they know how to make the baby and where did that baby find a mate?

15.   If one of the proven laws of science says that everything will break down over time unless structured energy is added. How did cells evolve instead of devolve before plants were capable of converting energy from the sun?

16.   Why can't they show any animals today with an organ or a limb in the process of evolving into something else. Like a lizards leg growing feathers preparing to become a wing?

17.   Why aren't there any fossils of creatures that are in the process of changing that show misshapen limbs. I.e. why are all the fossils fully functional animals? Shouldn't there be some record of the bad mutations since almost all mutations are bad?

18.   How did the ancestors of the first bird survive while their legs were useless for walking but incapable of flying?

19.   How did the first heart start beating at the right pace at the right time and hooked up to the right blood vessels? How did the creature survive while the heart was evolving.

20.   How come we still learn things that support evolution that were proven wrong years ago?

Like that there is a clear and orderly geologic column? - it would be over 100 miles thick if it existed.

Like Haeckel's diagrams of embryos? - proven a fraud

Like whales and snakes having vestigial legs? - used for reproduction

Like that our tailbone is proof that we used to have a tail? - without it we would struggle to poop or stand up

Like that our appendix is vestigial? – used by your immune system

- There have actually been so many 'vestigial' organs that have been found to have vital roles that they have started to claim that 'vestigial' doesn't mean without function. But most dictionaries still define vestige in biology as "a degenerate or imperfectly developed organ or structure that has little or no utility, but that in an earlier stage of the individual or in preceding evolutionary forms of the organism performed a useful function."
- Evolutionists changing their definition of vestigial is just one more example of how their story is never consistent!
- If it's got a clear function then it's not proof of anything but design. Check out this five minute video https://answersingenesis.org/human-body/vestigial-organs/

21   Why do we make simple things complicated?

Like all these crazy steps to get people on earth rather than just saying it was God.

Like that the earth must be billions of years old when the rock layers can be easily explained by a flood.

Like that the Grand Canyon took millions of years to form even though we've seen the Toutle River carve the "little Grand Canyon" overnight after Mt. St. Helen erupted?

Like saying that dinosaurs lived 66 million years ago when we have people throughout history describing them and drawing them and writing about them as real animals that they simply called dragons?

These are just a few questions… there are many, many more. Enjoy!

www.ingramcontent.com/pod-product-compliance
Lightning Source LLC
Chambersburg PA
CBHW041526070426
42452CB00036B/29